On the Go
Cars

David and Penny Glover

First published in 2007 by Wayland

Copyright © Wayland 2007
This paperback edition published in 2010 by Wayland

Wayland
338 Euston Road
London NW1 3BH

Wayland
Level 17/207 Kent Street
Sydney, NSW 2000

Editor: Camilla Lloyd
Editorial Assistant: Katie Powell
Designer: Elaine Wilkinson
Picture Researcher: Kathy Lockley

Picture Acknowledgements: The author and publisher would like to thank the following for allowing these pictures to be reproduced in this publication: Cover: Bugatti and Daimler Chrysler. Bugatti: 1, 17; Daimler Chrysler 2006: 2, 6, 7, 8, 9, 10, 15t; Mark Everleigh/Alamy: 12, Bubbles Photography/Alamy: 18t, Barry Bland/Alamy: 21; Liu Liqun/Corbis:4, Jose Fuste Raga/Corbis: 5, Erik Freeland/Corbis: 11, Paul Hardy/Corbis: 13, Don Heiny/Corbis: 14, Rick Gomez/Corbis: 17t, Murat Taner/zefa/Corbis: 18b, David Woods/Corbis: 19, Reuters/Corbis: 20; Chinch Gyniewicz/Ecoscene: 15b; Hulton Archive/Getty Images: 22; Rex Features: 16t.

With special thanks to Bugatti and Daimler Chrysler 2006..

British Library Cataloguing in Publication Data
Glover, David, 1953 Sept. 4-
        Cars. - (On the go)
        1. Automobiles - Juvenile literature
        I. Title II. Glover, Penny
        629.2'22

ISBN 978 0 7502 6154 8

Printed in China

Wayland is a division of Hachette Children's Books
www.hachette.co.uk

Contents

What are cars?

Cars are vehicles. They carry people from place to place.

People love cars! Cars are the most popular way to travel. There are many different types of car.

Sometimes there are too many cars.
Then they block the roads with
traffic jams. Many cars **pollute**
the air with **fumes**.

traffic jam

Car quiz
What is the most popular way to travel?

Car parts

Most cars have four wheels and a **bonnet** at the front. The driver looks through the **windscreen** to see the road ahead. **Indicators** flash when the car is turning.

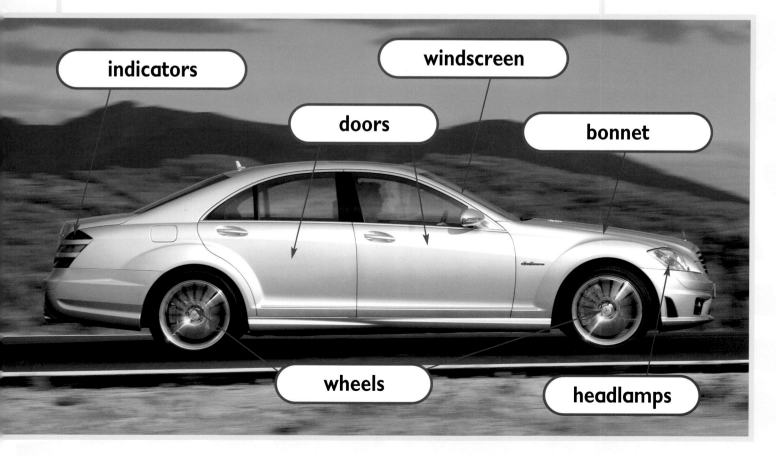

indicators

windscreen

doors

bonnet

wheels

headlamps

boot

luggage

brake lights

rear lights

The door of the **boot** lifts up at the back. There is space inside for luggage. The rear lights are red to show they are at the back. Brake lights warn drivers behind that the car is stopping.

Car quiz
What colour are a car's rear lights?

What is inside?

The driver and passengers sit inside. The driver steers the car with the steering wheel. The driver's feet press the pedals to make the car go and stop.

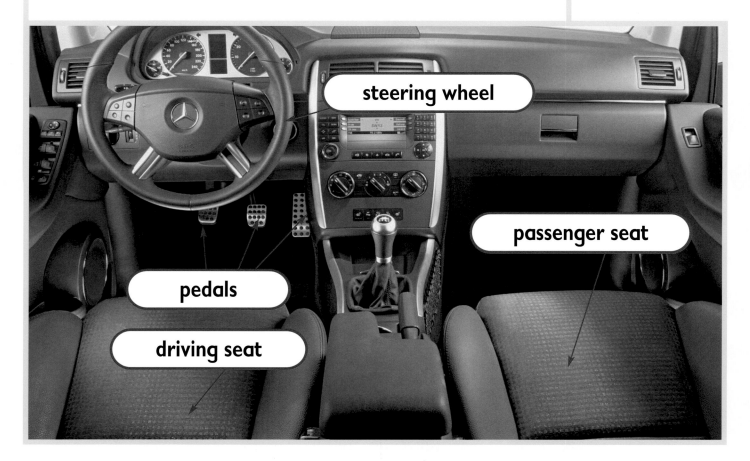

steering wheel

passenger seat

pedals

driving seat

dashboard

speedometer

gear stick

The **speedometer** is on the **dashboard** of the car. It shows how fast the car is going. The driver uses the gear stick to make the car go forwards and backwards and to change the speed.

Car quiz
How does the driver know how fast the car is going?

What makes it go?

engine

A car's **engine** makes it go.
The engine turns the wheels to drive
the car along. Most car engines are
under the bonnet at the front.

petrol

diesel

fuel tank

Car engines run on **petrol** or **diesel fuel**. The driver fills the fuel tank at the garage. The driver must put the right fuel in the tank or the car will break down!

Car quiz

What will happen if the driver fills the tank with the wrong fuel?

Working cars

A **four-by-four car** can climb steep hills and cross rough ground in the country.

Farmers can use four-by-fours to cross their fields easily.

Sometimes a police car must drive very fast. Then the police driver turns on the **siren**. The sound of the siren, and a flashing light, warns other drivers to move out of the way.

warning lights

Car quiz
Where can a four-by-four go?

Special cars

Sports cars have powerful engines and **streamlined** bodies like this Ferrari. Sports cars are very fast and expensive. They use a lot of petrol and must be driven carefully.

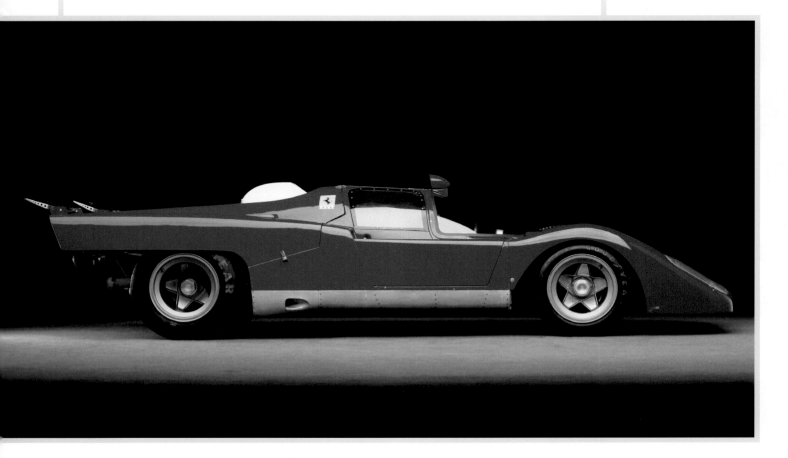

The Smart car is good for driving in the city. It can fit into a small parking place. Its small engine does not use much petrol. Some new cars have electric engines. They do not pollute the air with fumes.

electric car

Car quiz
Why are cars with electric motors good?

Record cars

The Thrust SSC is the fastest car in the world. It has two jet engines like a plane.

The Thrust SSC set a world land speed record of 763 miles per hour. That's faster than a jumbo jet.

Car quiz

What is the world land speed record?

Stretch limos are cars that are very long. The longest car in the world is a stretch limo with 26 wheels. It has a swimming pool and space at the back for a helicopter!

The Bugatti Veyron is the fastest car you can drive on ordinary roads. Some people think that it is the best car ever made.

Driving safely

seat belt

The driver and all the passengers must wear seat belts. In a car accident, a seat belt stops you from flying through the windscreen.

A car driver must always keep to the **speed limit**. Accidents are much worse when a car is travelling too fast.

air bag

dummy

If there is an accident, an **air bag** blows up to protect the passengers and the driver. Dummies are used to test the air bags.

Car quiz
Why do you wear a seat belt in a car?

Racing cars

Racing cars race on special tracks. F1 cars and Indy cars are the fastest racing cars of all. At the end of the race, the winning car is the first to pass the black and white flag.

Bangers are old cars that race around dirt tracks. No one minds if they bump into each other.

Car quiz

What does the winning driver see at the end of a race?

Old cars

The first cars were made about one hundred years ago. They were slow, bumpy and often broke down.

Car words

air bag
A soft bag that blows up if there is a crash to cushion the driver and the passengers.

bonnet
The lid over the engine at the front of a car.

boot
The boot is at the back of the car and has room for luggage.

dashboard
The place inside the car with the switches and speedometer.

diesel
The fuel that some cars use instead of petrol to make them go.

engine
The part of the car that makes it work.

four-by-four car
A four-wheel drive car that has good steering and control.

fuel
Something that burns inside an engine to make it work.

fumes
Dirty clouds of smoke that a car engine gives out.

indicators
Lights that flash to show which way a car is turning.

petrol
The fuel that many cars use to make them go.

pollute
To make dirty.

siren
A part of a vehicle that can make a loud warning sound.

speed limit
How fast cars are allowed to go.

speedometer
The part that shows the driver how fast the car is going.

streamlined
Smooth, like a sports car.

traffic jam
A line of cars that block the road.

windscreen
A car's front window.

Quiz answers

Page 5 By car.

Page 7 Red.

Page 9 The speedometer shows them.

Page 11 The car will break down.

Page 13 Up steep hills and across rough ground.

Page 15 They do not pollute the air.

Page 16 763 miles per hour.

Page 19 To stop you flying through the windscreen if there is an accident.

Page 21 The black and white flag.

Index